Dale Earnhardt Jr.

By Jeff Savage

AMAZING
ATHLETES

⌐ Lerner Publications Company • Minneapolis

Lerner Publications Company
A division of Lerner Publishing Group
241 First Avenue North
Minneapolis, Minnesota U.S.A.

Website address: www.lernerbooks.com

Library of Congress Cataloging-in-Publication Data

Savage, Jeff, 1961–
    Dale Earnhardt, Jr. / by Jeff Savage.
       p.   cm. — (Amazing athletes)
    Includes index.
    ISBN-13: 978-0-8225-2946-0 (lib. bdg. : alk. paper)
    ISBN-10: 0-8225-2946-7 (lib. bdg. : alk. paper)
    1. Earnhardt, Dale, Jr.—Juvenile literature. 2. Automobile racing drivers—United States—
Biography—Juvenile literature. I. Title. II. Series.
    GV1032.E18S28 2006
    796.72'092—dc22   2005003126

Manufactured in the United States of America
  3 4 5 6 7 – DP – 11 10 09 08 07 06

TABLE OF CONTENTS

Dale Earnhardt Jr.'s number 8 *(right)* car started out as the leader at the 2004 Daytona 500. But other cars soon passed him, and he had to catch up.

A WIN FOR DAD

Dale Earnhardt Jr.'s number 8 car roared past the **grandstands** at 190 miles per hour. Thousands of fans wearing Dale's red and white colors cheered him on. Dale was racing against dozens of other drivers in the 2004 Daytona 500.

The Daytona 500 is called the Great American Race. It is the biggest and most important race of the National Association for Stock Car Automobile Racing (NASCAR) season. The winner of the Daytona 500 would have a great chance to win the NASCAR **points title**.

Dale was eager to win the race. But he had more than a points title on his mind. Three years earlier, Dale's father, Dale Earnhardt Sr., had been killed during the Daytona 500 race. Dale wanted to win this race for his dad.

Stock cars are like normal cars except they have bigger engines. Drivers earn points based on how they finish in races. Points are added up at the end of the season to decide the points title winner.

Dale makes a **pit stop**. His crew changes his tires and fills his car with gas.

Dale Jr. is shy and carefree. His friends and fans have given him the nickname Little E. Since his father's death, Little E has become NASCAR's most popular driver. His face appears in TV ads and on magazine covers.

On the racetrack, Dale is a tough and smart driver. In this race, he had been chasing the leader, Tony Stewart, for 30 **laps**. Dale hung close to Stewart. He waited for the perfect moment to pass.

Dale finally got his chance with less than 20 laps to go. His number 8 car came screaming out of a turn. Dale zipped high on the track to try to pass Stewart. Stewart went high to block him. Then Dale dove low. He swerved within inches of Stewart's car to move alongside it.

Dale sticks close behind number 20, Tony Stewart's car. Stewart was the leader for much of the race.

For a second, the two cars were even. Then Dale gunned his engine and roared past Stewart. The grandstands shook. "I can't believe I passed him," Dale said, "It was like a magic trick."

The crowd goes wild as Dale zips past Stewart to take the lead.

Dale zooms across the finish line as a race official waves the checkered flag. Dale has won the race!

Stewart could not catch up. Dale crossed the finish line beneath the **checkered flag**. He stopped his car and climbed out. He removed his helmet and blew a kiss to the sky. He was crying. Then he got in his car again and spun circles on the infield grass.

Finally, Dale pulled into **Victory Lane**. His **crew members** were waiting. They lifted him onto their shoulders, and the crowd roared once more. "It feels like I'm closer to Dad," said Dale. "This is the greatest day of my life."

Dale celebrates his Daytona 500 win with his teammates and friends.

Dale *(left)* with his father, Dale Earnhardt Sr. Dale Sr. was one of NASCAR's greatest drivers.

LEARNING TO RACE

Dale Earnhardt Jr. was born October 10, 1974, in Concord, North Carolina. His mother's name is Brenda Earnhardt. Dale Jr.'s parents divorced when he was three years old. So Dale and his older sister Kelley lived with their mother.

When Dale was six, a fire destroyed his mother's home. Dale and Kelley went to live with their father in Kannapolis, North Carolina. Dale also lived with his stepmother Teresa. Later, his half-brother Kerry and stepsister Taylor Nicole joined the family.

Dale grew up around race cars and race tracks. His father was NASCAR's most popular driver. Dale Earnhardt Sr.'s tough, hard-charging style earned him the nickname the Intimidator. Dale's grandfather Ralph Earnhardt was also a top race car driver who won many races.

Dale's nickname was Junior. He loved watching races on TV.

Dale Earnhardt Sr. won the Winston Cup points title seven times. He is tied for the most points title with Richard Petty.

Dale's father let his son make his own decisions. "But he always had one eye on me," Dale said. After getting his driver's license, Dale and his half-brother bought an old 1978 Chevrolet Monte Carlo for $200. They fixed the car up to race. Dale wanted to be a race car driver for one reason. "I wanted to impress my dad," he admitted.

Dale's half-brother Kerry is also a successful NASCAR driver.

Dale Sr. did not want to help his sons too much. He wanted his boys to learn about cars and racing on their own. "He's got to learn it from the bottom up," Dale Earnhardt Sr. said. "How far up he goes is based on how much he learns." Dale Jr. was not allowed to race the car until he drove it for 150 laps. One day, Dale did so without stopping. "Well," his father said, "you didn't hit anything. Let's see how you do in traffic."

It didn't take long for Dale to show he was ready to be a NASCAR driver.

A ROARING START

Dale's racing career soared from the start. He started racing when he was 17 years old. Soon he was competing at tracks in North and South Carolina.

When Dale wasn't racing, he worked at his father's car dealership. But his favorite place was the racetrack. Meanwhile, Dale's dad kept an eye on him. Dale Sr. saw that his son was an excellent driver. He thought that Dale Jr. had a chance to be a success in NASCAR.

In 1998, Dale Sr. invited his son to join his team. Dale Jr. was about to get his chance to be a NASCAR driver! He started with the **Busch Series** racing **circuit**. The Busch Series is one step below NASCAR's top circuit.

Dale was nervous during his first Busch Series race. He didn't do well. In fact, he got into a terrible crash. His car did a flip and landed on its wheels. Luckily, Dale was not hurt.

But Dale learned from his mistakes. Just two months later, he won his first Busch Series

Dale Sr. congratulates his son for winning his second Busch Series points title.

race. He earned that first victory at the Coca-Cola 300 at Texas Motor Speedway.

Dale soon won again. And again. In fact, Dale won seven races. His great season earned him the 1998 Busch Series points title. He was the champion of his circuit! It was the first time in NASCAR history that a grandfather, father, and son had all won points titles.

In 1999, Dale won six races and the Busch Series title again. Dad was proud. "He had a lot of pressure on him," said Dale Sr. "He kept his head about him. He did a good job."

Racing fans expected big things from Dale when he joined NASCAR's top circuit.

Dale joined the top level of NASCAR in 2000. He was thrilled to race against his father and the best stock car drivers in the world. He drove with a yellow stripe on the back of his number 8 car. The stripe was a sign that he was a **rookie**.

Dale soon showed that he was ready for the top NASCAR circuit. He earned his first victory in his 12th race of the season. After winning the DirecTV 500 at Texas Motor Speedway, Dale's father greeted him in Victory Lane. It was an exciting moment for both father and son.

Dale won twice more in his rookie season. He had proved his skill behind the wheel. But some people said Dale did not work hard enough at his sport. He liked to go boating and hang out with friends. "I never told anybody that I was going to be as good as my dad," said Junior. "I just want to drive race cars and make a living doing it." But then something happened that changed Dale's life forever.

Dale and his dad pose for a picture before the start of a special race at Daytona International Speedway in 2001. Dale Sr. died in a crash at Daytona just a few weeks later.

MOVING ON

Dale's life-changing moment came during the first race of the 2001 season. The 2001 Daytona 500 was a fight to the finish. On the final lap, Dale Jr. was battling Michael Waltrip for the victory. Waltrip was in first place, with Dale right behind him. Dale's father was third.

Dale is strapped in and ready to race. NASCAR drivers wear helmets and special seat belts to keep them safe.

A Star Is Born

Dale grew more serious about racing. He shaved his beard and mustache. He ate healthy foods. "I want to prove there's more to me than just magazine covers and fun times," said Dale. "I think I'm a good race car driver."

Dale burns some rubber to celebrate another win.

Dale finished third in the 2003 **points standings**. He opened 2004 by winning at Daytona. And he kept on winning. At the Pontiac Performance 400 at Richmond International Raceway, Dale showed he knew how to drive like his dad. He boldly jumped on the outside of leader Jimmie Johnson and stormed past. "I'm normally not that aggressive with the car, and for just a second I felt like my daddy," said Junior. "It was kind of neat."

Dale went on to win four more races in 2004. He finished fifth in the points standings.

By 2005, Dale had earned almost $30 million in prize money for his career. He has a big collection of street cars and race cars. He also gives plenty of money to charities. Dale enjoys his life, but he is not satisfied. He wants to win a points title.

Dale battles Jeff Gordon *(left)* for the lead at the 2005 Radio Shack/ Samsung 500 at Texas Motor Speedway.

Dale's main focus is winning races, just like his father. "I don't compete against my dad's fame," Dale says. "I want to do everything I can to honor him. Part of me always wants to stay under Dad's wing. But there's a part of me that wants to break out and be my own man. I'm going to be champion. I have that confidence."

Dale gears up for another race. Racing is dangerous, but Dale doesn't worry. "I know when I go out there I could die," he says. "But if I quit driving race cars because of that, I wouldn't be living."

Selected Career Highlights

2004   Finished fifth in the Nextel Cup points standings
Won NASCAR's Most Popular Driver Award
Won the Daytona 500 at Daytona International Speedway
Won the Golden Corral 500 at Atlanta Motor Speedway
Won the Pontiac Performance 400 at Richmond International Raceway
Won the Sharpie 500 at Bristol Motor Speedway
Won the EA Sports 500 at Talladega Superspeedway
Won the Checker Auto Parts 500 at Phoenix International Raceway
Earned $8,913,510 in prize money

2003   Finished third in the Winston Cup points standings
Won Aaron's 499 at Talladega Superspeedway
Won Checker Auto Parts 500 at Phoenix International Raceway
Won NASCAR's Most Popular Driver Award
Earned $6,880,807 in prize money

2002   Finished eleventh in the Winston Cup points standings
Won Aaron's 499 at Talladega Superspeedway
Won EA Sports Thunder 500 at Talladega Superspeedway
Earned $4,970,034 in prize money

2001   Finished eighth in the Winston Cup points standings
Won the Pepsi 400 at Daytona International Speedway
Won the MBNA.com 400 at Dover Downs International Speedway
Won the Alabama 500 at Talladega Superspeedway
Earned more than $5,800,000 in prize money

2000   Finished sixteenth in the Winston Cup points standings
Won the DirecTV 500 at Texas Motor Speedway for his first Winston
   Cup victory
Won the Pontiac Excitement 400 at Richmond International Raceway
Won The Winston all-star race at Lowe's Motor Speedway
Earned $2,583,075 in prize money

1999   Won Busch Series title for second
   straight year
Won six Busch Series races

1998   Won Busch Series title
Won seven Busch Series races

Glossary

Busch Series: NASCAR's second circuit. Busch Series drivers hope to earn a spot in NASCAR's top circuit, the Nextel Cup.

checkered flag: the black-and-white flag that is waved at the end of a race

circuit: a racing league

crew members: people who build and repair NASCAR cars and trucks

grandstands: the area where fans watch a NASCAR race

laps: complete trips around a racetrack

NASCAR: the National Association for Stock Car Automobile Racing. Founded in 1947, NASCAR is the governing group of stock car racing. It says which changes to a car's engine and body are allowed to make it a stock car.

pit stop: a stop during a race in an area where a car can be fixed or gassed up

points standings: a list that shows how many points each NASCAR driver has earned. The driver with the most points is at the top of the standings. The driver with the second-most points is second in the standings and so on.

points title: an award given each year to the NASCAR driver who has earned the most points throughout the racing season. In NASCAR, drivers earn points for winning races, finishing well in races, and for other reasons.

prize money: the money awarded to each driver based on the driver's finish in a race

rookie: a first-year player or driver in a sport or league

Victory Lane: a road extending from the racetrack that the winning car drives along when celebrating a win

Further Reading & Websites

Armentrout, David, and Patricia Armentrout. *Dale Earnhardt Jr.* Vero Beach, FL: Rourke Publishers, 2004.

Gigliotti, Jim. *Dale Earnhardt Jr.: Tragedy and Triumph.* Maple Plain, MN: Tradition Books, 2004.

Kirkpatrick, Rob. *Dale Earnhardt Jr.* New York: PowerKids Press, 2002.

Stewart, Mark. *Dale Earnhardt Jr.: Driven by Destiny.* Brookfield, CT: Millbrook Press, 2003.

NASCAR.com
http://www.nascar.com
NASCAR's official site has recent news stories, driver biographies, and information about racing teams and stock cars.

The Official Website of Dale Earnhardt Jr.
http://www.dalejr.com
Dale's official website features trivia, photos, information, and occasional letters from Dale.

Sports Illustrated for Kids
http://www.sikids.com
The *Sports Illustrated for Kids* website covers all sports, including NASCAR.

Index

Photo Acknowledgments

Photographs are used with the permission of: © George Tiedemann/
NewSport/CORBIS, pp. 4, 7, 26; © Michael Kim/CORBIS, p. 6; © CHARLES W
LUZIER/Reuters/CORBIS, p. 8; © STRINGER/USA/Reuters/CORBIS, p. 9;
© MARK WALLHEISER/Reuters/CORBIS, p. 10; © Reuters/CORBIS, pp. 11, 20,
21, 22, 23; © Harold Hinson/The Sporting News/ZUMA Press, p. 13; © Brian
Cleary/Getty Images, p. 15; © Brian Cleary/Icon SMI, p. 17; © Duomo/CORBIS,
pp. 18, 29; © Jonathan Ferrey/Getty Images, p. 25; © Icon SMI/CORBIS, p. 27;
© JOE SKIPPER/Reuters/CORBIS, p. 28.

Front cover: © Sam Sharpe/CORBIS